cat ca

Published by the Fox Press
Main Road, Colden Common, Winchester
Hampshire SO21 1TL
Telephone & Fax 0703 694650

ISBN 0 9518743 1 4

No part of this publication may be reproduced, or used in any form, without prior permission of the publishers.

Designed & Printed by Southern Publicity Limited
Consort Road, Eastleigh, Hampshire SO5 4JB
Telephone 0703 619522

By the same author:

No Bitter Springs

First Aid for Wild Birds

Goblet of Delight

Poetry

Willow Seeds and Wild Roses
(Mitre Press)

Songs at Midnight

Where Trees Stand Tall

Cat Calls
an Anthology
Compiled and Edited by
Jeannette Arnold

with extra material by
Vincent Andrunas
Norman Goodland
Joan Howes
Jocelyn Jenkins
Lynette Watson

Photographs except where otherwise stated
by *Len Harvell* and the author.
Illustrations by *Jeannette Arnold*.
Also re-issued in this volume is
'Septimus Bumble'
originally published in 1982.

This is not a book for the cat expert or for those whose interests lie in the curl of a whisker of success or the show bench. All this, of course, has its place in the world of the cat - or perhaps, more correctly, in the world of the cat owner. No, this is an anthology about cats, cat owners, those who deal with both cats and their owners, cat poets - anything, in fact, both in ancient and modern times which is, or has been, concerned with these intelligent and beautiful animals.

Jeannette Arnold

Contents

Amongst a variety of observations, poems and anecdotes, you will also find the following contributions to this anthology:

Vincent Andrunas
Bouzouki   *30*

Jeannette Arnold
The Rehabilitation of Kingsley   *24*
The Birth   *65*
Septimus Bumble   *69*

Norman Goodland
Cat Supernatural   *40*

Joan Howes   *16, 18, 19, 37*

Jocelyn Jenkins   *64*

Lynette Watson
Bonaparte   *62*

Those who are concerned with animal welfare receive their fair share of telephone calls - sometimes curious, always interesting and often amusing. A selection of just such 'cat calls' is included throughout the following pages.

My cat knows every word I say.

Tibby is dead - long live . . . . . .

Our poor Tibby has died - we shall never have another cat.
About a week later:
We've just got another absolutely beautiful kitten.

My cat's claws are ruining my sofa - how can I stop him?
Is he Siamese?
Yes.
You can't.

Our cat has just had five kittens - the vet says he should be spayed.
Pardon?

Do you think my cat has got worms?
Sounds like it.
Ugggggh!

In ancient Egypt the cat was considered to be a sacred animal and Diodorus recorded that anyone responsible for the death of a cat - even if it was accidental - was put to death.

In medieval England a cat was enclosed in a bag and hung from a tree - the bag was then used as a target for 'sportsmen' to shoot at.

In England a male cat is called a 'tom' cat and a female cat a 'queen'.
In Scotland a male cat is sometimes called a 'Gib' cat and a female cat a 'Doe'.

So revered were the cats of ancient Egypt that the historian, Herodotus, records that should a building catch fire any cats inside would be rescued before the inmates since there could be no greater calamity than the death of these animals. When they died in the natural course of things great expense and attention was lavished on the funeral ceremony.

The goddess, Bast, was first represented as a lion goddess but later on she was known as the cat headed goddess. This goddess was associated with festivals and happiness. Any cats which had lived in the vicinity of her temples were regarded as sacred and were, often, mummified when they died.

Bast: Egyptian cat-headed goddess

Today, millions of cats, along with other unfortunate animals are used in the practice of vivisection. Attempts to justify this are made by those who perpetrate such atrocities since it advances knowledge which plays a part in the alleviation of human suffering. This, being interpreted on a personal level - opinions for or against vivisection can only be formed on a personal level in the final analysis - means ' I don't care about suffering as long as it is not my own'.

As *John Bryant* has remarked in his book *'Fettered Kingdoms'* published by Fox Press:

I once asked a thinking friend for his opinion on the use of animals for research. He replied: 'I would agree to the use of any animal if I thought it might save the life of my daughter'. I then asked him if he would agree to the suffering and death of, say, 50,000 monkeys if there were a chance it might save his daughter's life. He replied, 'Yes.' I told him that I could not accept that this was right and he quickly retorted: 'I am not saying that this would be right - I am saying that I would agree to it.' This supremely unhypocritical answer illustrates the dilemma in which Man finds himself. He believes his own species, particularly his own family or nationality, is of such importance that he would tolerate any suffering of animals if he thought it might benefit his 'own kind'. Surely this philosophy cannot be one of which the the human race can be proud?

Those who believe that such use of other beings is justifiable because we are 'superior' will be in real trouble if this planet is ever invaded by a superior being with similar morals!

Conversation with a Rex Cat

Henry - all eyes and red collar - perched compactly on my knee and warm as toast announced that he intended to put in a complaint. Interested I waited for more.
'I'm tired,' said Henry, 'of wearing a coat all winter and getting sunburned in the summer and I'm tired of people saying 'What's the matter with that one?'
He paused and then continued 'I've been thinking about it and when I go to heaven, which I confidently expect to do as I have led such a sheltered life, I shall put it to God that if he doesn't mind if I would like to come back as a Persian cat'. He paused again and then added dreamily 'A very, very, long haired Persian cat with a thick coat and proper whiskers too.'

From 'Shadow Shapes' J.A.

Siamese

Ruth and Flo are Siamese.
They do exactly as they please.
They do not respond to saying 'NO'
In stern, forbidding tones and so
If you would have a Siamese
Remember you will have to please
Its whims and fancies - cat desires -
Of being spoilt it never tires.
You'll be its slave so if you must
Own such a cat just
Heed this warning - 'twill be so -
As with Ruth and as with Flo -
As with all proper Siamese.
Your cat itself alone will please.

From 'Shadow Shapes' J.A.

The cats - paws, whiskers, tails
entwined,
Ignore with customary aplomb the
wrath
of Gods or men - and sleep -
scarce breathing, so deep and
unconcerned they sleep.

Extract from 'The Storm' J.A.

Who's that ringing at my doorbell?
A little pussy that isn't very well.
Rub its little nose with a little mutton fat,
For that's the best cure for a little
pussy cat.

Anon.

No Sex Please

My Siamese lady cat has gone mad -
she's rolling around on the floor and
yelling her head off.
Is she spayed?
No.
Well, she's yelling for a tom cat.
Nonsense. She's not interested in that
sort of thing.

Cat loving lady rather outstaying her welcome

I expect you just can't bear to let any of
these dear little pussies go to good
homes can you?
Oh - I don't know - I just force myself.

Gender Again.

You know our girl kitten.
Yes.
Well it isn't after all - it's my husband's
fault - he said it was the same as rabbits.

Ditto

How can I stop my cat eating my woolly jumpers ?
Is it a Siamese ?
Yes.
You can't.

How can I stop my cat peeing down the curtains ?
Is it a Siamese ?
Yes.
Is it a tom ?
Yes.
You can't.

That 'op'

Do I need to have my cat castrated?
Yes.
But surely that will interfere with his natural desires -
Mmmmm........

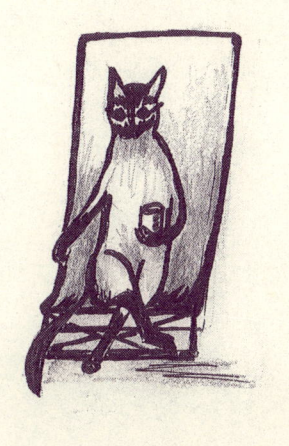

Home from Home

Do you mind if my cat brings his deck chair when he comes in for boarding?
Not if you think he'll feel lost without it.

See Previous

My cat catches birds. How can I stop him?
You can't.

Gus's 'Do'!

Augustus Gambit Moonmoth
Is a harbinger of style.
From non-Designer labels
He would frankly run a mile.
He wears his sable jacket
With a cool unstudied grace
And shows his noble lineage
In his bearing and his face,
Which carries marks of breeding
That set him on a plane
Apart from lessor moggies
Who make love in the back lane.
But come his birthday party
There will be no time for 'side'.
His paw amid the munchies
Will bear no mark of pride.
He'll cuff the first contender
To nab his catnip mouse
And fill the air with cuss words
That resound about the house.
Augustus Gambit Moonmoth
Will cast hauteur away
When finger-lickin' chicken
Is served to make his day.

He'll have a lovely birthday
With tasty treats and toys
And while he's making merry
He'll be just 'one of the boys'.
But with the 'morning after'
When the revelry goes flat,
Augustus Gambit Moonmoth
Will resume his Other Hat!

Joan Howes

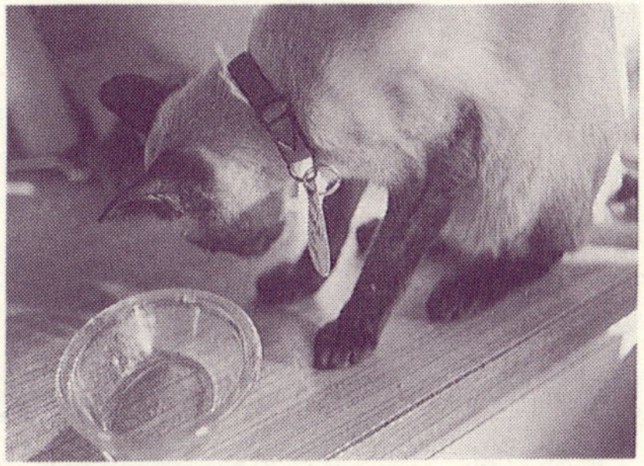

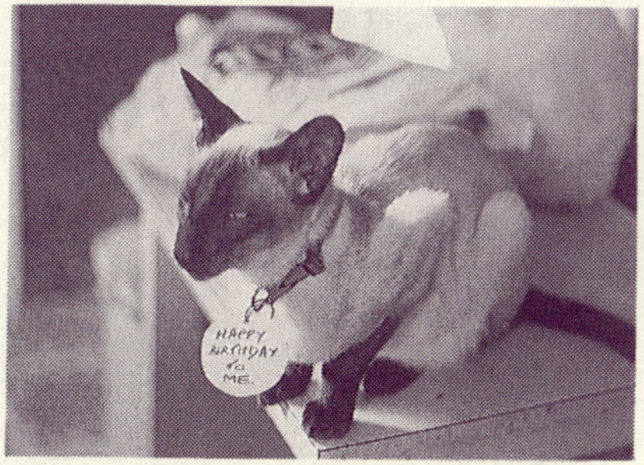
HAPPY
BIRTHDAY
TO
ME.

To an Enormous Cat !

Great chieftain of the moggy race,
Am I in permanent disgrace
For overstepping humour's edge
And hooting at your acreage ?

No lasting hurt was my intent,
No injury was ever meant
To leave such solid flesh in pain -
Whoops - sorry - there I go again !

Great warrior of the feline clan,
No homage could be warmer than
The admiration justly due
To one formidable as you.

A cat who plainly knows his worth -
And by an accident of birth,
Grew to proportions vastly more
Than God Himself had bargained for !

Joan Howes

One - Ear Rolfe

An ugly Bill Sikes of a cat
Who prowled our garden walls
With baleful stealth.
We hid our Mibs in the dolls' pram
When he sidled past,
His torn ear a sinister badge of combat.
Our nights were splintered
By the shattering music of his lust.
Our dustbins reverberated
From the zeal of his inspections.
Yet, he was held in half-amused
affection,
His square head reliably durable,
Like pre-war merchandise.
They say his people were bombed out.
I hope they thought to search for him
Beneath the rubble.
He was a natural survivor.

Joan Howes

God notices the sparrow's fall -
so we are told.
But having planned and introduced
the cat
It seems not to bother him at all.

If you were a guinea pig - rabbit or rat -
or even a cat.
You'd have different views on vivisection
pest control -
God and all that.

Detail from oil painting

'Not a sparrow falls...'   Jeannette Arnold. '91.

From the RSPCA magazine 'The Animal World' published in August 1903   Extract 1

We all know the expression 'cat and dog life' is used for a life of incessant, exasperating, petty warfare; but why should we not sometimes glorify expressions, instead of yielding to the general tendency to degrade them. A 'villain' once meant a valuable servant, a labourer on a 'villa' or farm; then let 'a cat and dog life' mean a life of pleasant ease and comfortable self-realisation.

I have made various feline and canine acquaintances whose lives have certainly been such, and it is amusing to recall their dainty whims and fancies.

There was one lady of the city of Edinburgh who spent her afternoons in dignified observation of the crowd in Princes Street at its junction with the Lothian Road.

She sat motionless on a horsehair chair, looking down calmly upon the crowd below from a fourth-storey window, her paws placed firmly on the sill. One could almost see the 'fibry frills' around her face, and could imagine her kindly comment on the passers by, and one could feel quite certain as to her attitude concerning Burke and Hare, Lord George Gordon and the building of the George IVth Bridge.

Her mistress was an invalid who kept her in her room but this did not make my friend yield a point of her dignity. She must have her seat at the tea table and her seat by the fire, whatever should befall. In the mornings, I fancy, she attended to her larder - old Edinburgh houses, no doubt, have good rooms attached and her toilet was not neglected for she had such a sleek, satisfied air as she sat, unfed, by the side of her mistress drinking her tea - though it is true she had her saucer of milk when tea was over.

And so she quietly lived her life of observation and household duty.

Extract 2 from the same publication

Both cats and dogs I fancy understand pretty well how to look after number one, more particularly the former, I think, for there is hardly a doubt that she is the more selfish creature of the two, the affection being chiefly cupboard love, and attaching herself more to places than persons. Not that I would exactly disparage her for this trait, it was given no doubt for a purpose, and she requires it to assert herself under rather difficult circumstances sometimes, for she is doubtless inclined to be overlooked. So she sticks up her back and moves about in a ridiculously superb manner, often remarkably overdone. She is credited with a special foreknowledge of, and behaviours during rain.
'While rain depends the pensive cat gives o'er
Her frolic, and pursues her tail no more'.
Shakespeare knew all about them both, thus in Hamlet we have :-

'Let Hercules himself do what he may,
The cat will mew, and dog will have his day'.
I fear puss, like the ladies, is given great licence and takes extreme liberties. They are, however, wonderfully clever at moving amongst the most fragile and crowded things without upsetting anything - just the reverse, in fact, to the proverbial bull in the china shop. A grand cat of my acquaintance, Bogie by name (peace to her ashes, alas, she succumbed to poison) was allowed by her young mistress to roam about the dinner table, and in and out among the maze of glasses, flowers, and dishes she threaded her way, steering with her magnificent brush without so much as ever disturbing the equilibrium of a single article.

These extracts are taken from a very tattered and ancient RSPCA book so that I am unable to give credit to the author(s) of these articles - the names are quite faded away.

The Rehabilitation of Kingsley

Kingsley's reputation, as with some human beings, had preceded his arrival. I had heard on the grape vine that he was a 'difficult' cat and reading in the local paper of the demise of his owner, I pondered for a moment as to his eventual destiny and then, being busy, I forgot all about the matter.
I had no idea that I was to be his eventual destiny.

Some time and several telephone conversations later I learned that he was confirming, in no uncertain way, his reputation and that he had been placed in the care of a very kind lady who owned a cattery, not too far away, while his future was decided.

The cattery staff confirmed that he was indeed, quite impossible and, despite their experience with all manner of cats, they would, to put it bluntly, prefer his room to his company. In any case, boarding fees were mounting and with the approach of the holiday season, the chalet was needed for prior bookings. I suggested - tentatively - in that manner when we are rather hoping that our offer will be appreciated but not taken up - that I should go and see him. The offer was immediately accepted and off we went.

Some little distance from Kingsley's temporary abode, I could hear him roaring out his views on the world in general and, as I approached, myself in particular. I did not push familiarity far enough to enter his pen and as I looked at this awful, very cross cat, I wondered what on earth was to become of him.

This time I did not forget about him and I felt in my bones that he was about to end up with us. And so it proved to be. My friend Ann and I collected him and arriving home, I put him in our own boarding pens and wondered, once again, what was to be done with him.

He was truly the most awful cat I had ever met - he roared incessantly at everything and everybody - he roared until his throat was hoarse or his vocal powers packed up altogether - the only time there was any respite for our ears.

If he attacked, he was not just threatening - he meant every scratch and spit - even putting his food down was fraught with danger unless one wore a glove. He had obviously heard about biting the hand that feeds...Kindly, cat loving people would peer at him, from a safe distance, and make soothing noises - he would respond to this by spitting, rolling his eyes and turning up the volume of his bawls and they would shake their heads and leave - no doubt feeling somewhat inadequate in their understanding as 'cat people'.

The situation continued with no change for about three months and I was beginning to question just what quality of life there was for this unhappy little creature which seemed unable to communicate with anybody or anything. Discussions with our vet brought us no further except that he pointed out that Kingsley could be quite capable of inflicting serious damage in the light of his present behaviour and, being a light hearted and realistic chap, he expressed the hope that he would not be on duty if Kingsley was ever taken sufficiently ill to need veterinary treatment as he (the cat) was obviously potty.

Then one day I took a deep breath and prepared myself for action - the situation had been static for too long. I removed my glove and held out my hand to him - he retreated, bawled, spat and raised his paw but did not actually launch into his usual attack. So far so good I thought. But, once again, that was the limit of any progress except that I had managed to obtain his permission to sit on a chair in his pen. And it was sitting here on a cold, rainy day feeling somewhat disconsolate and wanting my tea so that my mind was on things other than Kingsley's bad temper, that I felt a paw reach out and just touch my legs. I can be forgiven for saying that I stiffened somewhat with apprehension - after all I had seen Kingsley in action but - miracle of miracles - out came his other paw and very slowly, inch by inch, he crept on to my lap. I knew better than to touch him at this point and, after only a moment, he jumped off and resumed his bawling but I knew, and so did he, that we had made some kind of contact. It was a little too early to call it an understanding.

The next day Kingsley appeared keen to repeat the performance - on the understanding, of course, that he was doing me a great honour by allowing such familiarity. So, there I was with this bad tempered cat on my lap and totally unsure what his next move would be and then.........then I heard a low, rusty, grinding sound and I realised that he was trying to purr. It was as if he had not purred for so long that he had forgotten that this was something that cats did from time to time. It was a deep, painful, croaking noise which was endeavouring to proclaim that 'cheerfulness' had indeed broken in and I do not know which of us was more surprised - although, perhaps, Kingsley was more embarrassed than surprised.

The next day I decided that the time had come to put an end to his nonsense and, when he was off guard for a moment, I popped him into a carrier and dumped him in the kitchen into the fray, the 'fray' in this case being our own cats, Fred, Eppie and Joseph. Kingsley immediately reverted to his earlier, nasty self and spat and bawled at everything in sight. Fred, who had been taking a nap, opened one eye (he never opens both eyes when he first wakes up until he is sure that some emergency demands this) and gazed at this noisy intruder, got up and walked out of the kitchen and up the garden path and resumed his nap on the top of the garden shed. Kingsley was somewhat put about by this and bawled double strength at Fred's retreating back. How dare they ignore him ? Wasn't he the most awful cat in the world ? Hadn't everybody always said so ?

Eppie, in the meantime, sat with her tail curled, very neatly, around her toes - she was pondering about the intruder and she certainly did not like the noise he was making so she decided to do something about it and, being female, what she did was sensible and down to earth. She went up to him, sniffed his nose in greeting and then boxed him, very soundly, on both ears in rapid succession. Kingsley was affronted, surprised, taken aback, angry and visibly deflating like a punctured balloon. He went very quiet and gazing furtively around, he crept behind the boiler - he obviously wished for a little solitude and safety to meditate on his loss of face and his plan of action. But Joseph my young Siamese - still young enough to disregard the behaviour of cross, grown-up cats, strolled up and, chirruping a friendly greeting, poked his head behind the boiler as well. Not being able to see Kingsley at this point, I cannot record his reaction but it was not too grave because Joseph went on chatting to him and, finally, he too disappeared behind the boiler to sit with his new 'friend'. And that is exactly how it has proved to be - within a few days Joseph and Kingsley were inseparable buddies - Eppie has grown to love him and sleeps with him in an indeterminable heap. As for Fred, he has the odd chat with him but, this apart, it has not made any obvious difference to his amiable and peaceful way of life.

Kingsley ? Well, he has become a model of decorous, feline behaviour and, indeed, so completely has he erased his earlier lifestyle from his mind, that he finds any cat misdemeanours deplorable - and points his aristocratic nose firmly in the opposite direction. But Joseph, who does not lead an entirely blameless life takes advantage of that candour which can be exercised between true friends to point out that - it is all very well for him to take such a stand when he (Joseph) was actually bought and invited to live here whilst he (Kingsley) only came because he misbehaved and nobody else would have him.

J.A.

Bouzouki

Hello! My name is Bouzouki Pythagoras Andrunas. I am a grey tabby cat, and was born in the Autumn of 1986 in Athens, Greece.

When I was only a month or two old, I was abandoned in the National Gardens in Athens. Although very young, I was smart enough to quickly learn to compete for food with the other abandoned cats and kittens - there are over 200 of them there in the Gardens. On my first day there, I was seen by Mrs. Maria Liati, whom I later learned is a wonderful woman who has dedicated herself to caring for many of the hundreds of unfortunate homeless cats living in the Gardens. With Mrs. Liati on that day was Vincent Andrunas, a visiting American who likes cats. I couldn't understand what he was saying, because in those days I could only speak Greek. But I could tell he was friendly, and he seemed to have the makings of a good father (which was what I really needed!), so I made him fall in love with me by looking as cute and as smart as I could. Sure enough, he liked me so much that he came back every day to visit me! He wanted to take me home to America with him, but he thought he would have trouble getting me through Customs. Finally, he called the American Embassy and told them that he had a 'friend' who wanted to take a homeless kitten back to America. The Embassy personnel told him that it would not be a problem, as long as the kitten appeared to be healthy. No papers or examinations were needed; a cat need only look healthy to get through Customs and enter America. (Many people don't know this - if they did, I'm sure more of my friends in the Gardens would find themselves going to America like I did!)

Vincent bought a cat carrier at a local cat department store (they seem to call them 'pet stores' here...), came to the Gardens, and scooped me up. Off he took me to a veterinarian, where he had me checked, cleaned, and de'fleaed, and I got my first 'kitten shot' (ouch!). I stayed at the vet's for a couple of days, and then spent a night at the beautiful Grande Bretagne Hotel, just across the street from my temporary home in the Gardens. The hotel staff made me feel very welcome - the telephone operator, who lives with several cats, brought me a box with some kitty-litter, and brought a bottle of Ouzo for Vincent. The next morning, I was taken in a taxi to the airport, and we boarded a TWA flight. Vincent's companion, a textile artist, had made me a little Greek passport (but nobody ever asked me to present it, so I have no stamps to recount my travels!). After the plane took off, Vincent took me out of my little carrier and let me lie on his lap. The drone of the plane's engines made me so relaxed

that I slept through most of the flight, but I remember people in the airplane coming by and saying how cute I was, and Vincent telling them something about me. I later realised he was telling them where I came from and how we had met.

I felt fine when we left Athens, but as the plane began its descent for a short stopover in Paris, the pressure change made me feel a little uncomfortable. I told Vincent about it, but his Greek wasn't very good then, and somehow he thought I just needed to use a sandbox. So after landing, Vincent took me in my carrier through the Paris airport until he found a huge potted palm tree. He took me from the carrier and put me in the pot next to the tree. It was fun to dig in the dirt a little, but I really didn't need to go so I decided to jump down on the floor so I could walk around the airport a little - after all, it was my first time in Paris - in fact, it was my first time in any country other than Greece, and I was curious to see how the French cats lived. But Vincent quickly scooped me up and put me back in my carrier. Soon we were back on the plane, heading for New York City, where Vincent lived at that time. This was a much longer flight, but I just slept most of the way and hardly noticed the time. When we arrived in New York, Vincent put me (in my carrier) on top of a big pile of his luggage and wheeled me through Customs. The Customs Agent just kept looking at me and saying what a cute kitten I was, and how I had travelled so far for one of such an early age. He completely forgot to ask Vincent any embarrassing questions about what was in all those suitcases...

Vincent's apartment in New York was very different from anywhere I had ever been before. It was comfortable and warm, and there was good food to eat. I stayed inside all the time, except to go out on the terrace or when Vincent took me up to the roof garden. I was given the name 'Bouzouki' because when I speak I don't just say 'meow'; I make a sequence of sounds that Vincent thinks are somewhat 'musical.' The 'Pythagoras' part is in honour of John Pythagoras Samios, a wonderful Greek-American artist who is a friend of Vincent, and who also lives in the New York area. I quickly found out that whenever Vincent (or anyone else) calls my name - or my shorter nicknames, like 'Zouk' or 'Boogey' - it means I'm going to get something good, whether it's something to eat, or some attention and affection. Knowing that, I always respond, and come right away!

I liked living in New York City. Vincent immediately taught me the words for 'hungry' and 'eat' in English,

Photograph by Vincent Andrunas

French, and Greek, since those languages were spoken in the places I had visited or lived in. (Also, he thinks any well-educated cat should be able to understand those three languages.) He taught me to ask for things by sitting up straight and energetically waving my left paw. I soon learned that I could get just about anything from just about anybody by doing that, especially when they had something good to eat! If anybody says 'Sit up and wave' to me, I do it right away, and that really seems to make them feel good, somehow. Sometimes they even give me a tasty treat that Vincent calls 'candy.' (I found out that it's really just dry cat food, but it sure is tasty! Most of my food is of the canned variety, and I love it, but the dry 'candy' is really a treat for me!). The word 'candy' was quickly added to my fast-growing vocabulary. And although I was very wary of people in Greece - especially in the Gardens, where some people are very nice, but many others are very mean - now that I'm living with Vincent, I like everybody! Almost everyone that comes to visit has interesting things to say, an affectionate pat or stroke, or even some candy to share with me! So, of course, I'm always glad to see guests arrive.

After a couple of years in New York, Vincent moved to San Diego, California. Of course, he took me with him (I made sure he'd never want to leave me behind!). On the plane, the flight attendants asked about me, and Vincent told them where I was from and where I'd been. Later, they came back and offered to open a Frequent Flyer account for me, since I had flown more than most of the passengers they see! Life in California is especially nice; the weather is much like Athens, and I have a big yard to watch over, although I am still a house cat. Vincent says the streets are no place for a friendly, trusting cat like me. I'm not supposed to go outside at all without Vincent, but sometimes I sneak out to explore, or to chase other cats out of my yard. I liked learning things, and Vincent knew that with patience, persistence, and consistency, even a human can teach things to a bright cat like me. Soon he taught me to walk across a broomstick placed between the seats of two chairs. I sit on one chair, and wait to hear the word 'Walk.' Then I cross the broomstick to the other chair, and wait there. Learning and doing these 'tricks' is fun, and gives me a chance to earn surprised compliments (and oftentimes 'candy') from visitors. All someone has to do is say 'candy' and I get very excited! It's my favourite word, although I also know 'sit', 'down', 'stay', 'jump up', 'bread' (one of my favourite foods, though that often seems to surprise people), and all the other words I mentioned before. And now I'm learning to type on Vincent's computer, too!

If any other cats would like to know the secret to my happy life, it's that I have extended my kittenhood - I'm planning to go on being a kitten all my life! Vincent has made sure that I'll never need to learn to fight, or scrounge for food. Besides, I think I was really always meant to be an entertainer!

Vincent Andrunas
Courtesy of the
Greek Animal Welfare Society

Tail Talk

I'm having a lovely day.

I am extremely annoyed.

I am anticipating having a nice day.

Watch it - I've put my cap on and am seriously displeased.

I am pondering about life in general.

Outrage

She KNOWS what our favourite foods are,
She KNOWS we share delicate taste.
To set that old rubbish before us
Is not just an insult - it's WASTE !

She KNOWS we have sensitive tummies
That clamour for prime meat and fishes.
We saw her sly grin as she opened a TIN -
And unloaded it into our dishes !

We'll simply pretend not to notice.
We'd rather eat nothing at all.
To prove we deplore it, we'll simply ignore it-
And keep our gaze turned to the wall !

Joan Howes.

Postcards produced in the 1920's

Birthday Greetings.

A Birthday
happy, bright and gay
May all your
dreams come true,
And many
a happy
glad return
The future
bring to you.

To my Darling Little Grand-daughter Lots of Birthday Happiness.

Love,
joy and
hope,
three blessed
things
Be yours,
dear Child, where'er you go,
Filling your life with sunshine sweet,
Warming each hour with cheery glow.

A Happy Birthday
A Birthday wish for every gladness
May love and happiness entwined
Bring you years of every pleasure,
Health and best of Luck combined.
2216

Cat Supernatural

We were sitting in bed, having our nightly read before settling down to sleep. Our daughter Phillipa's car drew up outside.
That was nice. Even when they're grown-up, if they're in early - you can get off to sleep so much better. We heard the usual sounds. The back door. The living room door. Creak of stairs - click of the light switch.
'G'night.'
'G'night'.
'Have a good time dear...........?'
'Not bad...........'
Rustle of clothes. Clump of shoes on the carpet. Tinkle of trinkets on glass.
And then - an ALMIGHTY scream !
We froze - like two statues -
side by side.
A dishevelled half-draped figure burst in at the door.
'YOUR CAT! It shot out of the wardrobe. I nearly died!'
I said, 'We ALL nearly died. How did it get in there then ?'
'How would I know ? I HATE that cat! HATE IT! HATE IT!' And the figure disappeared.
We sat and giggled. He'd done far, far worse on us..........
Our wardrobe is beside the bed. A large, old fashioned heavy one with its door next to my wife.
One night we were having our read as usual - and we both looked up. The wardrobe door had moved. And as we watched, it slowly............slowly...........
... creaked open. My wife was rigid. I thought it a bit funny too.
'Do something'.
'Alright - don't get excited! It's only the cat!'
'Well put him out then. He must have been in there all day'. And what she said was worse than hating him. She said she was going to kill him.
But - there was no cat there. Not in the wardrobe, under the bed, in the spare

room - Phillipa's door was closed anyway: not in the bathroom, down the stairs - nowhere.
'Puss-puss-puss-puss-puss. Puss-puss. I thought - 'Where the hell are ye'. I thought - but didn't say it. Try talking rough to a cat -if you want it to come to you. But as I said - nothing!
I went down and made a great play of opening and shutting the front door as if I'd let the cat out. And then came up and back into bed.............
My wife read on for a while; switched out the light while I was in the middle of a paragraph as usual, thumped and bumped the pillows - got herself comfortable and was soon gone.............
But not me. I'd shut the wardrobe door again because Sylvia certainly wouldn't sleep with it open - and I lay there..................
There wasn't any cat. I lay there - listening.................
That door became a personality.

It breathed - through the dark. I found myself staring towards it. It appeared vaguely white - I could SEE it. It was going to move again - at any moment.............

I've an open mind about ghosts - and poltergeists - and things like that. But nothing further happened. Eventually - I did fall into a light and fitful sleep. But the ear that was cocked up in the cold stayed stiff and alert; like a sentry listening..................

'Miaow!' 'Miaow!' I sat upright - at once. Dawn was glimmering through the curtains.

'Miaow!' I slid out of bed. I rounded the end of it - and there was Cat. His black tail - straight up in the air with a little curl at the tip. His black face looking up at me. Trustingly. His green eyes round and shining. He turned and padded out of the door. And along the passage and down the stairs. With his dainty, two-fold duck-walk. Like a four footed ballerina. And I followed that straight-upright tail with its little curl at the tip his signal which said, 'Come with me'. Down to the front door - and the green eyes again stared up at me commanding - 'Open it!'

Which I did. And he duck-walked slowly out - and was gone.....................

Norman Goodland

Little Tiger On the Bed

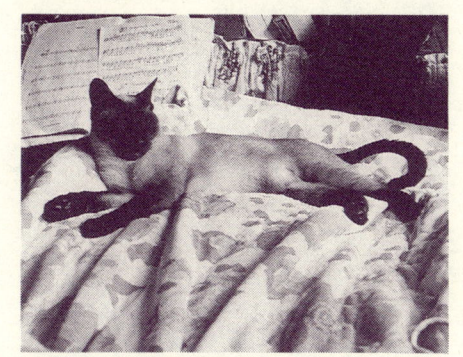

Little tiger on the bed -
What dreams and memories in your head?
Padding soft - eyes relentless
Power released - some creature lifeless.
Strength and beauty unaware -
No other living thing could dare
Challenge this - a blind authority.

Little tiger fast asleep
What dreams and memories do you keep?
Forest trees that touched the sky
Or hot sun where, replete, you lie
When, power released - some creature died
Which, careless, had no place to hide.

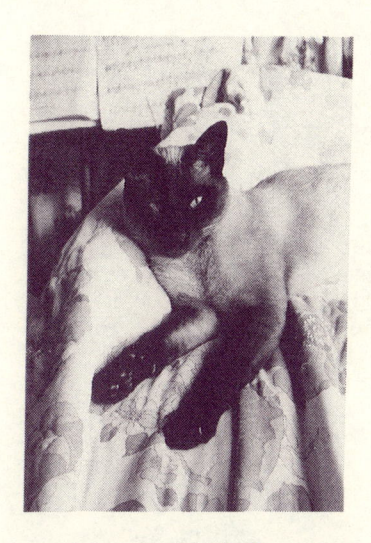

Little tiger on my bed
Come, shake such memories from your head.
Walk around this smaller world -
Leave the warmth where, cosy-curled,
My stroking hand will blunt such urgencies
And, claws in sheath, the world will see
A royal Siamese authority.

J.A.

Rescued Siamese

Pansy Helping to Make a Cake

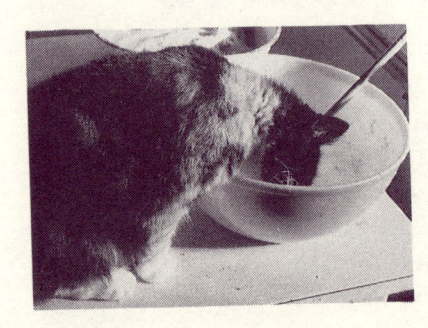

See Previous

My cat sprays down the door - how can
I stop him?
Is he Siamese?
Yes.
You can't.

My cat likes a saucer of Ovaltine for his
supper.

My cat suffers from constipation - I
hope you don't mind.
Not if he's happy about it.

Sequence

1

2

3

4

5

6

*Gus 5 months -
not quite grown into his ears.*

Gus. Now I'm really annoyed.

Punky - A Tortie Point Siamese.

Sandy Arnold with three generations of cats

Amicus

Owner of Fat Cat

You will remember to turn his plate round so that he can get to the other side won't you - if you don't he won't bother to walk round.

Is she really? I thought she was putting on a bit of weight.

My cat chews grass and then brings it up all over the carpet.

My cat spends most of its time sitting in the flowers.

My cat invites all his friends round now he's got his cat flap.

Our cat loves our Budgie.

Wrong Body

I've buried my neighbour's cat.
Pardon ?
Well, I thought it was ours.

O, you naughty boy - did you do that to
the kind lady ? Didn't I tell you he
doesn't like being groomed ?

My cat sprays down the curtains and it
changes colour.
Really ? What colour is he now?

Non cat loving husband to distraught
wife whose cat has gone missing:
'Well, I didn't ask him to go !

My cat keeps scratching.
Probably fleas.
O surely not, we live in a very nice area.

You remember me - don`t you ?
No - not off hand.
Yes you do - I brought you a stray
kitten about fifteen years ago.
Ah yes..........of course.

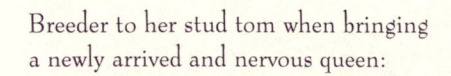

Breeder to her stud tom when bringing
a newly arrived and nervous queen:

Look Petey, here's a new girl friend -
O dear - don't do that ?
not straight away.

Luck of the Draw

My cat punches up my neighbour's cat.
My neighbour's cat punches up my cat.

Client to Cattery Owner

I expect you spend all day sitting with your little charges.
Cattery owner: Well, not ALL day.

What's In a name?

Old lady to companion:
This is where my cat comes for his holidays.
Turning to cattery owner:
This is my friend.
Turning to friend.:
Who are you?

My cat won't use his toilet tray if anybody is looking.

Told You So

Woman arriving in a damp skirt and wearing an aroma of tom cat:
My cat has just sprayed all over me in the car - do you think anyone will notice ?

My cat pees in the bed.

Passing the buck

Owner of cat coming for boarding:
Oh dear! He's had an accident
- I think he's sitting on it
- must fly
- can you cope?

Nasty People

Can you find a home for our cat ?
My husband says he puts hairs on his
blue suit.

Can you find a home for our cat? - the
children don't want him now he's
growing up.

You mean I just pop the pill down his
throat ?
Yes.
He's bitten my finger !

To owner of cattery:
Fancy that! He's not normally vicious.

Pen and ink sketch: Ellie & kitten

Bonaparte

Bonaparte was, indeed, a cat of great character who terrorised everyone for sixteen years. He was the most beautiful, longhaired tabby with an unbelievably evil temperament. The poor boy lost a back leg when quite young, but I do not think that this affected his nature as he commanded considerable respect even before that.

My elderly neighbour was terrified of him and, even towards the end of his life when his activities were considerably curtailed by arthritis in his remaining hip joint, he would make a great effort to drag himself over her wall so that he could play his favourite game. This involved nothing more than just sitting on the path by her outside lavatory (the only one she had); he considered it great fun to trap her inside (nothing would persuade her to walk past him; such was his reputation that she was convinced that he would leap at her throat);

however it was even more fun to prevent her from going in and I many times cringed with embarrassment as I heard her urgent wails.

We did not have a cat flap and he had twenty four hours access (he would not have tolerated any less) by means of an ever-open groundfloor bathroom window. This bathroom had a very flimsy sliding door which opened straight on to the kitchen and woe betide any unsuspecting guest who might want to use the facilities. He would make a special trip in especially to stare at them (one man complained that natural functioning was an impossibility in this situation) and when he had discomforted them enough (or more likely got bored) woe betide them once again if they didn't get the door to the kitchen open quickly enough for him. He had developed a flick of the paw that brought the bathroom door right off its runners (he simply pushed it away from him) and sent it crashing onto the cooker. The guest, no doubt wishing for the ground to open up, was then revealed enthroned to anyone who had come flying out to investigate the din.

My current cats are not a patch on him for ingenuity - he even discovered that if he stood on the pedal, the wastebin would disgorge its contents - chicken bones had to practically have a Securicor guard to the dustbin. Wonderful as they are, they are different and my Bonaparte can never be replaced.

Lynette Watson

To Boris

Black and lithe and yellow eyed,
soft paws patting at the door.
Climbing over, squeezing under,
watching birds above in wonder.
Singing loudly for his supper,
purring softly, sharp claws hidden.

No more frogs to trap and carry
no more frightened birds to catch
just the tattered leaves of lilies that he
loved to shred and play with.
Coalblack and young and yellow eyed
Please God, was . . . quick, the way
he died?

Jocelyn Jenkins

Birth

The little cat rose and stretching each delicate paw, padded silently and purposefully toward her box. As she walked her sides bulged and swayed - her time had come and instinctively she began to prepare for the birth of her kittens. Methodically she shredded the newspaper, arranged the piece of sheeting to her satisfaction, and then giving a little chirp, she lay down first this way and then that as if to find out which was the most comfortable position. For a while she stayed inside the box, not quite sure of what was to come but then almost unconcernedly she was out again enjoying a wash in the sun.

Quite suddenly she returned to her box only this time she lay down, she raised her hind quarters a little and bracing her feet against the side she began to strain.

This first effort soon passed and she got out once again and come over to me, purring and rubbing against me as if to say that she was pleased not to be alone.

Soon she was straining again and gradually the spasms came quicker and quicker until the little cat cried out in pain and effort to bear this, the first kit, which seemed to be wedged in the birth canal. At last she gave a mighty heave and a head appeared looking monstrous and distorted in the membrane of birth. Still she strained and pushed for what seemed an eternity to both of us; her eyes were wide and dark with pain. Then suddenly, with an almost audible pop, the kitten emerged completely. Swiftly the little cat turned and tore the sac from the face of her first born and as she did so, its mouth sighed open to take in the life giving air. She quickly and efficiently removed the remainder of the membrane which enveloped the kitten; the action of her rough tongue in doing so both washing him and helping him to keep his very new hold on life. Then chewing her way solidly through the afterbirth she finally broke the cord which had been her lifeline to her baby, now out of the warmth of her womb and protesting strangely and feebly at first - then more vigorously, struggling blindly for something that was as yet unknown to him. The little cat purred gently to him all the while and guided him to her nipple, which was to be the fountain of his comfort for some weeks to come.

Then the spasms were on her again and I took the little one from her, wrapping him in a warm blanket away from her struggling body - she would not mean to harm him, but she had no thought at this moment but to expel the next kitten. More quickly this time, the second little mite was born and she lay for a while with two babies in the shelter of her paws.

Soothing and praising the little cat, I offered some warm milk and this she lapped eagerly and gratefully. We both knew that there were more kittens to come, but for a while she lay resting and regaining a little of her strength. The spasms started again-and-again-and-again and, as I watched, I wondered as I have done so often before, why it was that the Lord of the universe saw fit to place this agony of birth on the female of most species.

Then it was all over, and lying side by side, suction attached to her nipples lay five new babies. The little cat looked up at me and there amidst her blood, weak from her efforts, and already drowsy with sleep, she closed her eyes until they were the merest slits and I could swear that she smiled at me.

From the Mortal Cold J.A.

Cat Fan

I think cats are blooming marvellous.

And so do we.

Finis.

Acknowledgement is made to The Estate of the late Edna St Vincent Millay for the inclusion of the final verse of 'Dirge Without Music' in the story of Septimus Bumble.

Septimus Bumble

1 New Arrival

Bumble came into my life almost eleven years ago. He came with no pedigree, it having been lost somewhere along the line in his movements from house to house. He was also without references as to his good character - indeed his unenthusiastic owners left me in no doubt at all about that, issuing dark warnings to 'watch him'. He had, it seemed, bitten everyone in the house - even the children. Knowing Bumble as I do now, I suspect that he had especially bitten the children.

He had arrived at my cattery to be cared for whilst the latest in his series of owners went on holiday - a leggy, somewhat morose looking seal point Siamese, about six months old and with a tail which was about half as long as is considered to be acceptable by those people who are qualified to make such judgements.

His arrival coincided with the height of the boarding season so that, being busy, I paid no more and no less attention to him than to any of the other cats which were temporarily in my care. It was only when his owners called to collect him that I noticed a certain hesitancy on their part to enter his pen - cat and cat owners seemed to stare at each other with a less than lukewarm appreciation of their reunion. I realised then, that here was something which I had never been able to resist since the arrival of my very first Siamese many years ago - a Siamese cat at odds with the world. I do not mean to imply that non-pedigree cats when in distress feel their unhappiness less acutely - simply that Siamese, because of their intense, and in many instances, slightly neurotic natures, require a special sort of understanding. Some of them are not suited to be first cats in a household, needing owners who have learned by experience how to bring out the best in this particular breed. This solemn, aloof and rather lonely looking kitten seemed to me to be just such a cat.

The lady was looking at me as if she was about to say something which had been rehearsed. I waited - I knew exactly what was coming.

'I wonder - ' she said. Then she began again. 'Do you ever - ?' Then finally in a rush: 'do you think that you could find a home for him? You see we don't really want him back!'

Then, out it all came - the story of Bumble's series of unsuccessful homings.

His name, incidentally, at that time was Ho-Tung and it appeared that he had been born of a mother who, like some human ladies we all know, was rather over zealous in her passion for tidying up - so much so that having given birth to her litter of kits, she cleaned both them and herself so assiduously that she inadvertently chewed off a fair portion of his tail. Not possibly the best way for a kitten to begin his sojourn in the world - to be expelled straight from the warmth and safety of his mother's womb to a direct demonstration of the sharpness of her teeth. Any kitten under such circumstances could not really be blamed for thinking if you can't trust your own mother you'd better start learning how to spit pretty quickly.

At any rate his tail deficiency had left him a slight liability to the lady who had bred him since he could not be considered a perfect specimen. So Bumble became a 'present' cat. He was given free of charge to some friends who were too polite to say thank you very much but we don't want a cat. Here he stayed for a while before being passed on to other friends and other friends of friends until he had arrived with this particular family. All of whom he had bitten.

Bumble had, by this time, divorced himself from the whole situation. He sat with his back towards us, his ridiculous little stump of a tail hanging over the edge of the window seat. Deeply engrossed in the antics of a small fly which was trapped in a spider's web, he made it quite clear that it was all one to him if he should stay or go. Despite his 'Billy The Kid' reputation there seemed to be an innocent unawareness of his inability to become loved which was, I suppose, the reason I found myself saying:

'Yes, don't worry. Leave him to me and I will do my best to find a really suitable home for him'.

The lady heaved the proverbial sigh of relief and she and her husband exchanged one of those glances which married people are prone to do in public - wrongly imagining that the message which has been transmitted is obvious only to themselves.

I had interpreted the message exactly. It said 'Thank God for that, let's get out of here before she changes her mind'.

They beamed at me and shook my hand and I felt an embarrassment at the compliments which were showered upon me and then, without even a backward glance at poor Bumble, they left. As they walked up the path I heard the lady say, 'Now we can get a proper kitten for the children'.

Proper kitten indeed! I supposed that they meant a kitten who would never scratch under any circumstances, which would eat when it should and purr when it should - a toy kitten which could be thrown away when interest had waned would probably do just as well.

With these uncharitable thoughts I returned to the pen which housed the kitten for which I was now responsible.

We looked at each other. It would be nice to relate that we were impressed - a kind of mutual recognition that Fate had brought us together but it was not so. I saw just an odd looking, unfriendly little Siamese - and Bumble, well he just looked at me in a manner which was completely devoid of any interest at all. It was almost as if he looked through me.

'You'd better behave yourself my lad,' I said '"otherwise you'll be for the chop.'

I didn't mean this of course but I felt that we might just as well start as we meant to go on which was, as far as I was concerned, tantrums from Bumble were out.

He did not even glance at me as I left his pen.

2 No Takers

Bumble settled happily into life in his pen, seeming to regard it as his own little home in which he could do as he pleased. He appeared not to expect any overtures towards friendliness and certainly none on his part were forthcoming.

He slept in the sun or under his heater according to the vagaries of the weather. His food was eaten with relish and, as with most appreciative cats, his plate was left polished and shining, the area both around it and underneath it having been well sniffed to make quite sure that he had not left a morsel.

He occasionally allowed himself a little amusement with a falling leaf or moving shadow or attempted a clout at a passing bee but it was done with a half-hearted, world weary air. He seemed, somehow, a very old kitten.

He used his tray cleanly and modestly - he was, in fact, the perfect boarder - albeit a non-paying one.

Contrary to the notions of the uninitiated, it is the aloof, undemonstrative cat which is easiest to care for under boarding conditions and not the one who showers its favours on all and sundry. Such cats tend to be very demanding in their constant need for affection, and while it is very understandable that each animal is, in the eye of its owner, the most important one in the cattery, collectively to the proprietor, they are all as important as each other - no more and no less.

Their aim being to return the cats to their owners in a healthy, and hopefully, happy state it is necessary to devote a great deal of time to the more menial tasks of scrubbing out and disinfecting the premises, thus the actual handling of the animals is kept to a minimum both because of the time factor and to avoid the transference of disease from one cat to another.

It is, I think, preferable that a boarder returns home suffering from a slight lack of affection - a deficiency which will have no lasting effects and is soon remedied by its owner, than to succumb to the possible diseases which can occur through a lack of hygiene. These may be not quite so easily put right.

My hopes that someone would see in Bumble the cat of their dreams were beginning to fade. He certainly did not put his heart into being someone's chosen one and when I tried to introduce him to a possible owner, he would back into a corner with his stumpy tail fluffed out, his ears lowered and a deliberate frown on his face. To this day he still frowns if he is displeased about something or other.

One lady, after gazing at him for quite a long while, said that she didn't think she would take him because he looked as if he 'thought things'. I knew exactly what she meant. Bumble can look at you with a complete lack of expression on his face which is most disconcerting, seeming as it does to hint of deep, dark, unfathomed cat thoughts.

At any rate, none of the people who were keen to become members of a cat owned household seemed anxious to further his acquaintance, even when informed that he was free. They would leave instead with one of our own bred kittens - prim little misses or cocky young toms, all of whom behaved exactly as young kittens should and who

assured their new owners that they intended to be a credit to them.

Eventually, the time came when I could no longer allow Bumble to remain in his pen, it being needed for incoming boarders. This meant that he would have to be integrated with our own resident cats - on the whole an amiable selection, although having a tendency toward racialism in that any cat which was not a Siamese was beneath their notice.

My particular favourite at that time was Huffy, a blue point tom which had come to me as a stray some years before but now, at the age of thirteen, his kidneys were failing fast. He had such a gentle nature and his illness so taxed his strength that I knew he would not be concerned with the advent of a new kitten.

Foxy, on the other hand, also a blue point, was quite another matter. He had been found wandering in the Southampton area, living the life of a complete drop-out; of no fixed abode, he had mended his ways a little but he still retained a great taste for fisticuffs and also, I regret to say, he never lost his skill in ' acquiring ' things from other people's houses. Any refrigerator which closed by suction was child's play to him, and I once caught him in the kitchen giving a demonstration of his skills in this direction, surrounded by a group of wide-eyed, admiring lady cats. I had no doubt at all that Foxy would notice Bumble 's arrival.

My other two toms were seal points. Charlie, then about twelve years old was, I believe, the most beautiful animal I have ever seen - his long slender body delicately shading from cream to honey fawn and dark seal brown was always a visual delight to me. Unfortunately poor old Charlie's brains did not match up to his looks and he was really as thick as two planks. If he decided when he met Bumble that he was friend then I knew it would stay that way - and if he decided otherwise so it would remain. I am not sure if it was more difficult to get an idea into his head or to get one out of it. Sometimes it seemed impossible to do either.

Tid, the second seal point, suffered from nerves and on this account excused himself from practically everything. In any argument he always considered that discretion really was the better part of valour.

The rest of the family were females who knew exactly how to deal with any upstart kittens and therefore presented no problem.

This then, was to become Bumble's family. When I brought him in from the cattery and set him down in the kitchen, I realised that he was now one of us - our kitten instead of a kitten in need of a home.

To set the seal on it I decided to rename him. I had never cared for the name Ho-Tung. It did not seem to suit him and also there was no satisfactory diminutive one could derive from it.

Naming a cat should never be done hastily. My husband and I decided to give the matter considerable thought.

3 Settling in

Bumble's arrival in the house proved to be something of a non-event.

Poor old Charlie, bemused as ever, thought he had probably miscounted in the first place.

Tid, given to hiding beneath the loose covers in the armchairs when any occasion warranted such action, took up his position there - just in case.

The girls, none of whom were gifted with more than their fair share of intelligence, were never quite sure whose kittens were whose, so they let the matter slide for the time being.

Foxy, intimating that he had an interesting day planned, had left quite early.

I had an inkling of what those plans had been when a rather irate neighbour appeared on my doorstep carrying two very dead guinea pigs. The insinuation was that Foxy was to blame, which I had no doubt he was but loyally I pointed out that if one kept these poor little animals in outside runs, one should at least make sure that their accommodation was such that predators could not gain entrance. Foxy was no magician (and here I crossed my fingers) and if he could get in - supposing that it was his handiwork - then so could other animals. The man was not wholly appeased.

The trouble was that where our Foxy was concerned, it was a case of 'give a cat a bad name'. His cheeky escapades had made him quite notorious in the village and any punch-ups, thefts or, as in this case, unlawful killings were invariably attributed to him. He was,

however, always open to discussion about his misdeeds if not wholly convinced by the arguments put forth.

On one occasion, I had noticed him enjoying himself at the expense of a terrified mouse and after rescuing the little creature, which appeared to be unharmed, I proceeded to lecture him, pointing out that the mouse had as much right to be under the willow tree as he had himself. Foxy sat on his haunches, gazing at me out of his beautiful blue eyes and listened intently. His eyes were particularly striking even for a blue point which, to my mind, is the colour point possessing the loveliest eye colouring.

The following morning he appeared at the kitchen door carrying a live mouse which, when dropped at my feet, couldn't believe its luck and without questioning its apparent favour in the eyes of the Almighty, it sped to the nearest cover.

Several minor furniture removing sessions were necessary before it was recaptured and returned to its natural habitat - all of which Foxy watched with extreme interest. He felt, I think, that he was really to be congratulated on having provided me with the means to partake in such a splendid game and was only waiting for me to finish when I would tell him what a good cat he had been. It occurred to me that although he had not quite taken in the real meaning of my lecture, at least he had not killed the mouse so I mustered what signs of approval I could manage and off he went with an airy wave of his tail which quite clearly said 'That's all right - any time.....'

For a while I was inundated with presents of mice until he went off the whole idea and no doubt reverted to his old habits. I did feel that it was all getting a bit out of hand when, on one such morning, he brought me a quite exceptional gift in the form of an adder, its forked tongue darting viciously as he prodded it delicately toward me.

On the morning of Bumble's arrival, soon after the departure of the gentleman with the dead guinea pigs, Foxy came heading for home with some urgency and I concluded that he had probably returned to the scene of his earlier crime and that the aforesaid gentleman had made his feelings clear about the matter.

At any rate, the result was that Foxy spent the rest of the day being a 'good' cat - thoroughly manicuring his nails, washing right down to the tip of his tail, etc. In short, doing all those little jobs with which home loving cats are wont to occupy their time and which he normally considered to be rather 'sissy'.

So occupied was he that he did not notice Bumble staring at him from beneath the sofa where he had retreated to consider this new turn of events, so that some time elapsed before Foxy's ears detected a slight sound coming from that corner of the room. He pondered about it for a moment and then poked his head under the sofa to investigate, thus coming eyeball to eyeball with Bumble. He simply could not believe what he saw - he had ceased to patrol his patch for a few hours due to adverse circumstances, only to find that some strange cat had somehow sneaked in and was even now sitting under his sofa.

He was too big to get under it so he fluffed himself out until he looked twice his normal size and proceeded to roar the most dreadful things at poor Bumble. Did he not realise that he had one hell of a cheek (Foxy's language was never anything but virile and masculine - you could, for instance, call him a cat but never a pussy cat) and if he didn't get the hell out of it pronto, and here he listed all the most awful things he could think of that he would personally 'do' to this usurper.

Bumble stayed as he was - there was not much else that he could do and as the sofa was against the wall, just so long as he did so there was not much chance of Foxy's threats coming to fruition.

After some considerable time, when running out of both breath and ideas, Foxy quietened down a little and contented himself with trying to outstare the cause of his wrath. He probably did not succeed in this because in later years, in any outstaring contest in which Bumble takes part, he is always the winner - bland and unwavering he is the 'champ'.

Finally, Foxy got fed up with the whole situation. Added to which he felt he was losing face so he left the scene of combat and pretended that he was much more interested in going to sleep in the sun.

A little later, due to a cramp or nature calling, Bumble crept cautiously from beneath the sofa, in a flash Foxy was across the room and, rising on his hind legs, with a quick bit of the old one two, he boxed Bumble soundly on both ears at once.

Bumble neither retreated nor retaliated. He was, after all, still a kitten and no doubt remembered enough of his mother's teaching to refrain from arguing with a mature, male cat. He simply frowned at Foxy and flattened his ears.

Now, our Foxy was undoubtedly a rascal, but a lovable one for all that and the lack of retaliation from Bumble caused him to pause for a moment, seeing then that it was only some upstart kitten he had encountered.

He began a new discourse but it was much less feverish and more of 'this hurts me more than it hurts you' type of lecture.

He pointed out, I think, that bed and board he could have but he must not at any time get above himself, he must not pinch the best cat seats or open the fridge door unless Foxy said so. He must never steal from Foxy's plate and finally any bits of crackling he encountered around the place were Foxy's.

Foxy's enthusiasm for the ladies had only been slightly dampened by a visit to the vet. It was now more a question of going through the motions, but as far as our ladies were concerned he still had what it takes to make a girl happy. It was rather like being on the pill I suppose - the sweets without the bitters.

Actually, Bumble needed no warning on this last subject. Neither before or after neutering has he ever shown the slightest interest in female cats and even now is deeply shocked when certain overtures are made to him by lady cats which are in season. When he puts his beautiful great head into a box of newly arrived kittens he is completely astounded by the whole thing. He knows that the girls are very often surrounded by these little, yelling nuisances but finds it all very mystifying.

Gradually, the cats accepted Bumble or perhaps I should say that they tolerated him for he made no friends and really did seem to walk alone.

Very often our cats will sleep curled up together in an indistinguishable, pulsating mass of ears, legs, tails, etc., but Bumble sleeps sedately on his own- the ottoman in our bedroom finally becoming his accepted sleeping place.

All through his life, no one but myself has ever cuddled him or handled him and it sometimes seems to be a great responsibility when one is the 'only' person to another living creature.

But for the time being, at any rate, Bumble seemed quite content with the situation. He still resented being handled at all but perhaps because he was in a home where he was not the only cat, not so much was expected of him, and if he wanted to remain aloof, well, being busy and having plenty of other cats about the place, we had no objection.

4 Death of Huffy

The weeks passed and still our addition had not acquired a name. This was partly due to the fact that 'kitten' talk to him seemed not to be appropriate and therefore no personal nickname came to mind but also at that time, I was preoccupied with the sadness of knowing that Huffy, my old blue point was rapidly losing his frail hold on life. One morning I discovered him hiding under the bed and in great distress and on examination I found an ominous swelling at the point of his jaw which was obviously an abscess.

This is one off those situations which one hopes will never arise in the case of a cat with malfunctioning kidneys and I knew that I could not ignore it. His teeth had needed attention for some long time now, but our vet had not been prepared to take the risk of administering the anaesthetic necessary in order to remove the tartar which is the almost inevitable accompaniment of kidney disease.

So it was, at nine-thirty the following morning with a great unhappiness, I took Huffy to the surgery, knowing in my heart that this was the end - one way or the other. As I came into the house about three-quarters of an hour later the telephone was ringing. It was Norman, our vet. It appeared that Huffy's reaction to the anaesthetic had been very bad indeed - even worse than we had anticipated and it was only when he was totally relaxed and deeply unconscious that the reason had been discovered. He had developed a carcinoma of the lungs and this along with his failing kidneys had been the cause of his rapid decline. Norman told me that he could, if I wished, bring Huffy round again and he estimated that he would probably live for a further six weeks or so but the quality of his life during that short time would be very poor.

I hesitated, feeling that I could not give the order for the destruction of this trusting old cat and yet the ordeal of suffering for him was already over. Why bring him back to go through it all again? All Norman needed to do was deepen the anaesthetic.

I heard myself saying: 'Do as you think best.' Then Norman's quiet reply, 'You know what I think.'

I put the receiver down and visualised the routine which would now be taking place at the surgery and wished I was without this familiarity of routine. Later on we collected Huffy and buried him in the woods - in death he seemed to weigh nothing at all.

Lying in bed that night, listening to the whispering of the trees in the woods, I thought that we did not have much of a choice as to what we did with the remains of the people or creatures that we loved. I thought of Huffy in the cold, dark earth and was reminded of that lovely poem by E. St Vincent Millay.

'I am not resigned to the shutting away of loving hearts in the hard ground
So it is, and so it will be, for so it has been, time out of mind:
In to the darkness they go, the wise and the lovely.
Crowned with lilies and laurels they go: but I am not resigned.
Down, down, down into the darkness of the grave
Gently they go, the beautiful, the tender, the kind:
Quietly they go, the intelligent, the witty, the brave.

I know. But I do not approve. And I am not resigned.'

Perhaps it was the loss of Huffy which made me look towards this new cat which I had acquired. Certainly I had a little more time to devote to him now that the daily routine of caring for Huffy was no longer necessary. Still, an appropriate name for him eluded us. Then one day he became Bumble.

We had noticed for some time that he had a habit of suddenly going round in circles and seemingly attempting to attack a point just beyond the tip of his stumpy tail, and had assumed that, as is the case with people who have lost limbs, he occasionally experienced sensations in that part of his tail which had been chewed off. During one such session my husband casually remarked, 'Look at that cat going round like bumble-bee' and that was that - Bumble he became.

Because he was such a dignified cat and also because he was the seventh Siamese which had belonged to me, I added the name of Septimus. I thought it had a nice ring to it and would make up for his loss of pedigree name.

Oddly enough he responded almost immediately to this name which he had never done when addressed as Ho-Tung. For myself, I was glad that he was at last registered as one of us.

5 Cats v Vets

It was beginning to be obvious that Bumble considered himself to be my cat - he was not particularly affectionate but wherever I was he would not be far away and I was often conscious of his bland, unwavering stare as he watched me at work. Sometimes he would sit on the stool in the kitchen purring so softly that I would only be aware of this by the slight tremor in his throat, gently disturbing his fur.

He had gained too, the respect of the other cats, not because he had proved himself to be stronger in a physical way - although he showed signs of the large cat he was to become - but rather because he had a presence which somehow deterred them from taking liberties with him. Should they think to steal from his plate he would lift up his head, pause, and stare at them without blinking until they crept away feeling very abashed. I was always reminded of the crushing looks given by some concert musicians should a member of the audience cough or otherwise make his presence obvious.

On the other hand should he feel that physical action was necessary he was more than capable of holding his own, placing his blows deftly and confidently, completely assured that he was always in the right - never in the whole of his life has it ever occurred to Bumble that he could possibly be wrong!

Of course, no respect was due to him from Foxy who, in his cheeky confident way, respected nobody so that a clash of opinions between the two of them needed to be nipped in the bud before something really serious developed. Foxy did, I suppose, respect the vet, or at least he regarded him as the sort of human being that it was best to avoid, remembering no doubt that a slight impediment had been experienced in his affaires with the ladies after their meeting.

I remember Norman - a man not noted for his placid temperament - informing Foxy that he was about *to be given a worm pill* and that he did not expect there to be any nonsense. He duly put the pill down Foxy's throat and waited for him to swallow - without the aforesaid nonsense. We both waited - and waited - Foxy did not swallow. He began to have a blue tongue and Norman to have a red face. I, trying to be helpful and wondering just how long a cat could survive without breathing, remarked that Foxy's tongue was turning blue. To which Norman, redder than ever of face, replied: 'So it may be, but he's going to swallow this . . . . pill.'

After what seemed a very long time to me Norman let go of Foxy and rubbing his hands together as people are wont to do after a job well done said: 'There you are you see - you've just got to let them see that you mean business - pill's gone.' Whereupon Foxy, complete with blue tongue jumped off the table, ran up the path and, disappearing in to the woods spat out the pill.

He was never one to harbour a grievance though and he reappeared later that evening cheerful as ever having completely forgotten the episode of the pill he didn't take.

Bumble, at that time, had experienced few veterinary procedures apart from neutering which, since it was done whilst he was still immature had had very little effect on him. I was not yet to know that in later years his behaviour when being treated by a vet either at home or at the surgery was to make Foxy's reputation that of an angelic cat by comparison. Indeed scrawled across the top of his medical card in Norman's untidy hand, as a warning to the uninitiated who in their innocence might have tried 'nice pussy' tactics, were the words - 'this cat is to be handled with caution'.

Many years later when it was considered necessary that a blood sample be taken to ascertain the exact degree of the severity of his kidney function disorder, I was greeted by a young and rather shy veterinary assistant who handed me my cat, now bawling his head off at the indignity of being confined to a cat carrier, together with a message from Norman - an explicit message which read - examination impossible - blood sample impossible - cat impossible.

Meekly I left the surgery with my, as ever, unpopular cat who concerned not at all with the state of his kidneys or my loss of face, purred all the way home, confident that he had behaved in the only possible way.

During the last seven years Bumble has needed a daily intake of kidney tablets and fairly frequent injections, both of which when administered by myself he has accepted with no resistance whatsoever. Sometimes when pilling him I may be a little clumsy so that it does not point directly down his throat and when this happens he will juggle it himself until it finally slips down. He assumes for some reason I think it necessary that he should go through this peculiar ritual and therefore he does not question it.

About this time Bumble and I were beginning to build a solid foundation for our partnership - although it was not something which could be hurried. He had developed a habit of sitting on the arm of my chair in the evenings or when I was resting.

Then came the time when he cautiously stepped on to my lap, not as most cats do, with their heads facing away and paws cosily tucked under, but confidentially with his face only a few inches from my own. Without thinking, having lived with cats for so long, I put my arm lightly around him - in a flash his paw was out and it landed straight in my face.

Taken somewhat by surprise and also feeling that his action was totally uncalled for, my reaction was immediate and uncompromising. Bumble blinked but he did not move or retaliate. Instead he sighed - not a sad sigh - rather a satisfied one and then settled down, closed his eyes and went to sleep.

He had recognised if not a boss, at least an equal, and never from that day to this has he raised a paw to me.

6 Tantrums

all other folk are quite de trop
he's no-one's cat but mine.

It was quite by accident that I discovered Bumble was a natural car traveller. One evening we had decided to visit my father and noticing that Foxy was in early and asleep on the sofa, I thought it might be unwise to leave the two of them together for a long period, so, on impulse I decided to take Bumble with us.

From the moment we were settled in the car he made it quite clear that he loved travelling - everything which he saw from he window was of interest to him and when he tired of that he settled himself on my lap, purring as he rarely did at home. As the car gathered speed or rounded corners he would steady himself by digging his claws into my legs so that I quickly learned to travel with a fairly thick cloth spread on my lap when Bumble was with us. Over the years he has become a seasoned traveller, regarding the car as his second home and a place to eat lots of cheese biscuits - a special delight to him.

He is always provided with a tray of sawdust should the journey be a long one and likely to include an inconvenient call of nature. In this I feel he is somewhat luckier than we humans who, when on our motorways, seem to chase will-o'-the-wisp lavatories forever posted as seven miles ahead!

A master of balance when engaged in this particular task, he manages at all times to keep the relevant parts poised over the tray despite speed or sudden swervings.

All holidays are planned with Bumble in mind and he is quite unmoved by people staring at him through the car window -

he simply returns their stares in his unique, unblinking, fashion - eyeball to eyeball, quelling at birth any possible 'pussy cat' conversation.

So Bumble grew from a leggy, morose young cat to a larger than average male of uncertain temperament seemingly unable to either take or accept friendship from anyone other than myself. My attachment to him was growing all the time and I would often fly to his defence, endeavouring to point out to others that he really was a very intelligent and affectionate cat but this was usually received without interest and with disbelief. Still, it seemed that nobody liked him very much.

There was one memorable occasion when Bumble and I arose after enjoying a Sunday afternoon nap feeling somewhat sleepy and stupid and there came a knock at the door. It turned out to be a nice 'catty' lady wishing to book her cats in for boarding. Bumble, who while not being a sociable animal, nevertheless was always quite interested in knowing what was going on, therefore appeared at the doorway prepared for a listen in. Without more ado the lady squeaked in that peculiar voice which some people use when talking to animals:

'Oh! what an adorable pussy!'
Nobody EVER called Bumble a pussy.
'Oh,' she continued, 'aren't you beautiful - I do love you and I am sure that you love me too!'
Here, the lady glanced in my direction and told me that all animals loved her because she loved them.

I did not feel too sure about this.

Bumble frowned - he was beginning not only to not love this lady but to actively dislike her.

I was just about to issue my usual warning that it might be better not to pick him up when the words died in my throat, for she had swooped on Bumble and was holding him in a tight embrace close to her face.

I had the distinct feeling that something not nice was about to happen - even now I am a little hazy as to what actually did happen. There was the most awful spine-chilling noise coming from the object of her 'love' which brought my husband at top speed from the garden thinking that someone was being murdered. Indeed, he was not far wrong because I think that Bumble had, at least, the intent to murder - he just had not quite thought how it was to be done. He had struggled from her grip and with his paws on her shoulders, claws digging in and his nose against hers, in the most appalling voice ever heard from any cat (even a Siamese)

was stating the most uncomplimentary remarks imaginable. Even such a devoted cat lover as this lady undoubtedly was, could no longer be deceived into thinking that Bumble loved her really.

I reached out and took a handful of him at the scruff and base of his tail and was glad that I had sufficient experience of animal work to know something of the best way to deal with animals of 'vicious intent' - as Bumble was at that moment. I literally has to prise him off and when he finally let go, with a final spit at the object of his 'non-love' he walked with great dignity up the garden path.

The incident was not quite finished with. Everybody started apologising to everybody else - except Bumble of course. He obviously felt that if the lady had not picked him up (which he had in no way intimated that he wished her to do) he wouldn't have got annoyed and so nothing would have happened. How could he possibly be to blame under those circumstances?

As the lady watched him walk away she said sadly and somewhat inadequately, 'Oh dear'.

As she did so Bumble turned round and giving her a look, walked purposefully to a nearby bush. It was as if he had suddenly had a good idea. Turning his back to the lady, his tail quivering poetically he performed a spray of such range and magnificence that it just missed her leg.

There was not much that I could say after that which was effective in restoring her ego with regard to her, until now, ability to communicate with all cats. I launched frantically into some kind of discussion drawing on my experience with cats - which, I assured her was quite considerable - and explained that there did exist certain cats which really were one-person animals and as such they strongly resented being handled by strangers. In fact, I continued, warming to my subject, even my husband would never attempt to pick Bumble up unless it was absolutely necessary. But somehow it all sounded as if I was reciting from a textbook and I bade her a sad and ashamed farewell. I suppose as is the way of things, she at that moment could not remember all those cats who probably did love her - only Bumble who didn't.

I decided that this time Bumble really had gone too far and that his behaviour warranted a good telling off - if not a good clout and with such intentions in mind I awaited his return.

About ten minutes later he came into the kitchen, slit-eyed, purring and loving. He wore his ears, as he often did, slightly cock-eyed thus giving him the appearance of The Laughing Cavalier - without the laugh. At least, I had always thought it was without the laugh but as I came forward preparatory to beginning my lecture, he lifted up his head and brought his nose to mine in such a conspiratorial manner and with such a twinkle in his eye that I found myself starting to laugh - the more we laughed, for Bumble was laughing, the more could I see the funny side of it. My husband coming into the kitchen at that moment gazed with disapproval at this apparent lack of sensitivity on our part and used to the amiable predictability of his 'ladies' announced that 'that cat' needed to be taught a lesson. I told him that to me, Bumble was quite beautiful which prompted the reply that beauty obviously really was in the eye of the beholder.

Although this was the first time that Bumble had actually attacked anyone, it was not the first time that he had expressed an opinion as it were, and on recollection I now see that in both instances it was to the same type of lady.

The previous incident had taken place during a visit to tea of another devoted cat lady who, although she admired my other cats seemed to be very desirous of winning Bumble's approval. Coyly she told him that she did not believe he was really as naughty as his reputation might lead her to think, and that underneath he was just a lovely big boy - the same as other cats.

Personally, I have always believed that the reputations we earn for ourselves in life are pretty accurate but I had noticed that as far as Bumble was concerned he was beginning to be regarded as the Gilbert Harding of the cat world - as if the unsociable side of him was just a cover up for the lovely him lurking beneath.

Bumble listened, unmoved and unblinking, as she continued to woo this mythical 'him'. Then slowly, as if he had all the time in the world (which I suppose he had really, surprise being the best form of attack I believe) he strolled over to her large red plastic bag which she had lodged against her chair and, gazing soulfully up into her face, he spent a small penny over it - a small, lingering penny. It in no way compared with the magnificence of his later garden effort but it was almost as effective - the lady concerned deciding that he really was rather nasty after all.

It is quite noticeable now, how tidy people are with their belongings when visiting our house and for myself, even during the most interesting conversation I keep a wary eye on Bumble's movements, abruptly ushering him out of the room if I should notice a thoughtful expression in his eyes as he gazes enigmatically at our visitors.

7 Cat Flu

When Bumble was about three years old, we, my husband, Bumble and myself returned home one Saturday afternoon having completed the weekly shopping. As we entered the garden gate we had no premonition of the bombshell which was about to explode in the midst of the settled life of our cats.

Placed in a prominent position against a low wall was a wicker basket with a note attached to it and all the rest of our cats were busily sniffing around it. The note said that the writer was quite sure that I would be able to find a home for the kittens which she had 'rescued'. It is always surprising to me that people can imagine that they have rescued an animal merely by asking someone else to find a home for it.

I opened the basket and my first reaction was extreme anger that some anonymous do-gooder should have placed such a lethal cargo amongst my animals - for inside were two small grey kittens both of which showed symptoms of virulent cat flu.

Neither my husband or myself wasted time in allowing our anger to explode. We isolated the kittens as far as possible from any other cats and disinfected the area where the basket had stood. We both realised that these precautions were probably too late but it seemed important to do something however unlikely that it would help what had been done.

We could then do nothing but wait - incubation for this disease was usually about seven days and our only hope was that our own cats would have met this particular strain of flu before and possibly have gained some immunity to it.

As the days went by we alternated between hope and despair. Exactly seven days later Foxy sneezed, quite lightly and unimportantly and under normal circumstances I probably would not even have noticed it, but he continued to sneeze on and off for the rest of the day. The next day he was still sneezing only not quite so often. The following day he was not sneezing at all.

We became cautiously optimistic as the days went by. Then one night I awoke to an odd sound which, with a mind still befuddled with sleep, I was unable to place. Becoming wide awake I realised that the noise was coming from Bumble - he was breathing in a very odd way indeed. Each respiration was broken rather like that of a child who has sobbed himself to sleep. I woke him up but it made no difference - still the same odd, broken breathing.

Now that he was awake Bumble himself knew that something was wrong and he sat in a sternum position in an effort to breathe normally. His eyes were wide and anxious.

I was relieved to find that although there was obviously a reason for this odd breathing there did not seem to be any actual difficulty in the intake of air. I lay awake impatiently waiting for the morning to come in order to contact Norman, who when he arrived said that it was too early to make a definite diagnosis. It could be the onset of cat flu or possibly some other respiratory infection. We would have to wait and see what further symptoms developed.

We did not have to wait long. By the following morning all the classic symptoms of cat flu had arrived in a particularly virulent form.

Bumble's eyes were running, his nose blocked and saliva in long streamers drooled from his mouth. His breathing was worse than ever.

I had seen this disease often enough to know that there is no treatment as such - the vet simply attempts to alleviate symptoms as they arise plus the administration of antibiotics to ward off any lurking secondary infections. With the complete loss of appetite which is part of cat flu the animal very soon loses condition and it is then that further complications are likely to set in.
I realised just how much this odd cat now meant to me and I was sick with apprehension.

Two days later Kerri our little twelve-year-old seal point lady began to sneeze - then Charlie and finally Tiddy.

The house appeared like a battlefield with our invalids lying around in various stages of distress. They seemed to make no progress at all and we were worn out with worry and lack of sleep, for it is most important that sick cats should be attended to during the small hours. It is then that their little spirits sink very low and it is then that they will die. One night I slept longer than I had intended and on waking I found Charlie semi-conscious on the floor, with the chill of death already in him. I took him in bed and placed him between my husband and myself and gradually a little life returned to him. Lacing a little warm milk and glucose with a few drops of brandy, I managed to get a few drops down his throat with the aid of a syringe. I was later to wish many times that I had let nature take its course for he was then fifteen years old and his slender old body was ill suited to withstand such a vicious onslaught of disease.

Bumble remained suspended in a state of depression which left him completely devoid of appetite and interested in nothing at all. It was some pointer to his condition that he allowed Norman to examine him with no protest whatsoever. He would sit for hours at a time, his head hanging and his body heaving in an attempt to breathe through his almost totally blocked nostrils. How many times I wished that I could have explained to them that if they opened their mouths as we humans do when we have a cold, they would have been able to breathe more easily. As it was, all I could do to afford them some relief was to wedge my fingers between their jaws so that they had no choice but to breathe through their mouths. This was very time consuming and my husband and I would take it in turns to be 'on duty' for this.

Bumble's skin folded over his bones in the manner of an outsize garment on a coat hanger, his fur was staring and lustreless and it seemed to be too much of an effort to turn his head to me - only his eyes would follow me about the room.

He felt, I think, that I was letting him down somewhat in not putting right whatever it was that was making life so unpleasant for him and I realised how wide the barrier between us really was in terms of communication in the accepted sense.

All I could do was keep him clean and cheer him up as much as possible. This is a most important aspect in the nursing of sick cats - especially in the case of the Siamese where the degree of depression is sometimes out of all proportion to the severity of the illness. One literally has to talk them back into a willingness to live or fight back.

Tiddy who, when he succumbed, was convinced that he would die almost immediately on account of his nerves was, in reality, much less affected by the disease than the other cats. I was not unduly concerned for his eventual recovery.

Kerri, on the other hand, had developed an ominous cough - deep seated and frequent, it racked her tiny body.

Then, one evening, I noticed that for a cat who was as ill as she was and who was eating so little, she gave the odd impression of having gained weight and this puzzled me. I picked her up and gently ran my hand over her and as I did so my heart was very sad, for with every movement of my hand on her body there came a tiny crackle rather like static electricity. It was coming from inside. I looked across at my husband for Kerri was his special favourite and what I had heard told me that she was dying.

It was a condition which I came across sometimes in injured birds but I had never until now seen it in a larger animal. When the respiratory system is damaged in some way, with each breath taken, air leaks out and slowly builds up in the body - rather like a slowly filling balloon.

I told my husband what I suspected and we stayed beside Kerri as much as we could that night, knowing what the morning would bring.

At eight o'clock the following day Norman arrived and after listening very carefully to her chest he began to fold his stethoscopes away very carefully, without looking in my direction - I knew what this meant.

He began then to prepare for what must be and very soon Kerri was no more.

Meanwhile the kittens who had been the innocent cause of the disaster were recovered and thriving in the homes which we eventually found for them - for all I know they may well be continuing to do so.

But I could not rejoice in their happiness. The price we were paying was too high.

8 Recovery

As January rained into February and the tentative sunshine of March appeared, the symptoms of flu began to disappear but it now remained to pick up the pieces and try to offset the after-effects, temporary or permanent of such a protracted illness.

Charlie had eaten nothing of his own accord for seven weeks and had been kept alive on a mixture of Complan, glucose, Brands essence, and injections of vitamin B12. At regular intervals Norman had introduced fluids beneath the skin to prevent dehydration. It was a day of great rejoicing when he took his first sips of glucose water and we felt that the battle might yet be won, but it never was. He lived a further year but the illness had broken him. He never again breathed normally and he died of a stroke soon after his sixteenth birthday.

Bumble began to eat again very slowly but the life seemed to have gone from him and he still sat for long periods doing nothing at all. Frequently he would vomit the small amount of food which he did manage to eat.

As the spring became more urgent and beautiful, I would carry him wrapped in a blanket through the woods and we would take him for short rides to those places which he had once enjoyed visiting, but it was heart-breaking to see him trying to take in interest and the effort involved proving too much for him, and he would sink into my lap with a bowed head. It seemed that the old Bumble had returned and it was all one to him of he should live or die.

Then, one day, in the course of my work I was preparing to take some urine samples to the surgery. On impulse I added Bumbles's, thinking that perhaps something could be gained from so doing. I knew that a negative sample does not prove conclusively that a cat does have kidney failure but a positive result certainly proves that they have.

Later that afternoon Norman telephoned to report that Bumble's sample was heavily positive. Well, I thought, at least we have something definite to go on now.

Immediately he was put on a strict diet and kidney tablets were administered three times each day. The injections of B12 at intervals were restarted. Slowly, very slowly it appeared to be working - the vomiting ceased and he began to put on a little weight. Gradually he became, once more, my larger than average cat and he began to take his old delight in travelling.

Since that time Bumble's diet has consisted of cooked meat with a dash of Marmite gravy. He occasionally eats a little boiled fish, although this is always under protest since he is not a 'fish' cat. Sometimes I allow him some item which may not be good for him just as a but only in very small quantities - in the main nothing is allowed to interfere with his diet.

His illness had the effect of making him more than ever my cat and even less tolerant of people than he was before and in the years that have followed I have left him only once - when I was myself rather hurried into hospital. Apart from the fact that he would not allow anyone else to 'pill' him, I feel that with the advancing years his kidney function would be seriously disrupted should the routine which we have followed for so long be altered in any way.

9 Just Bumble

Bumble always enjoys his pleasures in what would seem to be rather a melancholy fashion and in this, he reminds me of a friend of mine who when people feel sorry for him because he looks sad, replies, thank you very much but I am not sad - I just do not have a happy face. So it is with Bumble.

At the age of almost eleven years he is now undisputed head of our resident cats - a position which he holds with great dignity.

Tiddy, still assuring everybody that he is a martyr to his nerves, has happily renounced his claim to this title and with it all responsibility for everything. Despite his nerves, at the ripe old age of sixteen, like many another creaking door, he manages to survive through it all.

Foxy died at about thirteen years old, much as he had lived - doing it his way.

He came home one evening looking a little the worse for wear and I thought that he had probably met his match in one his still frequent punch-ups, but the following morning he was severely ill and despite the attention of the vet he died that same morning of a heart attack. Sad as I was to see his still, blue form and to realise that his beautiful blue eyes were closed to us for ever, even as the tears gathered in my own eyes, it was not difficult to imagine our Foxy, now sporting celestial wings on his way to chat up the keeper of the door to cat paradise.

Bumble is still a larger than average cat - particularly so for a Siamese and this together with his aloof air endows him with great presence , although it is with sadness that I see the signs of approaching age.

It is only I who know him him when dignity is not quite so apparent - when for instance he is sitting on the mat and I am whizzing him round and round. During this particular enjoyment he manages to give the impression of some religious dignitary letting his hair down at the fun fair - without actually losing the look of a cleric. Although, now I come to think of it, I am not sure which of us looks the more foolish.

There is an unconscious humour sometimes in the things that he does which springs from his assumption that the world and myself exist only for his particular enjoyment and it is at such times that he bestows a severely disapproving and uncomprehending look in my direction as I dissolve into laughter.

Visitors, seeing a large sleepy cat on our sofa tend to perch alongside thinking, no doubt, that that is the end of the matter, but after only a little while it is quite usual to see them start suddenly as Bumble's powerful hind legs and claws find their mark. Their reaction is commonly to say: 'Oh dear, did I sit on you' and then to move away which is, of course exactly what he had in mind.

Tiddy as had been pointed out before suffers from nerves. You must bear with me if I tend to repeat this statement but Tiddy does rather go on about his nerves. Well, the fact is he also nourishes phobias of several sorts. One such phobia is that he cannot eat with the other cats and further, he must not be seen by them when he is eating. I solve the problem by putting his plate under the bureau - the fact that his behind protrudes and is clearly visible to us all has apparently never occurred to him.

Now, on occasions, Bumble rises in that state of euphoria which assures him that he is about to have a lovely day - and how better to start such a day than to be offered something delicious such as roast chicken for breakfast. When he is offered something more homely such as boiled coley, he graphically mimes his reaction to such an offensive item by endeavouring to put it under the carpet. As if this is not sufficient to make his feelings clear about the matter, he is then wont to catch sight of Tiddy's behind protruding from the bureau. After a deliberate inspection of this he delivers a hefty whack at it before taking himself back to bed in a huff.

Oddly enough, Tiddy ignores the whole thing completely. I suppose he is secure in the knowledge that as he can't see the others they can't see him so that he thinks he imagines the impact of the whack.

Bumble does have one, so far unfulfilled ambition. When I take my bath which he always regards as an act of complete madness on my part, as the water finally gurgles down the plug hole, he will jump into the bath and gaze up at the taps and then longingly at the last of the water. It is then that I firmly remove him - I am sure that in common with some small boys who cherish similar ambitions, he would like to spend a penny exactly down the plug hole!

He believes, absolutely, in not going back to nature. He is all for central heating, civilised food and toilet trays. His opinion with regard to cows and their untidy habits when expected to walk across a field dotted with 'pats' is quite obvious.

He has not the slightest desire to be free, to be a cat who walks alone, to fend for himself or to be allowed to roam at night - the very idea of such a thing impels him to hurry indoors lest he be shut out accidentally.

Yet for all his unreliability where human beings and other cats are concerned, he has never in his life been responsible for the death of another living thing - at least not to my knowledge.

Mice are not creatures which he meets at all frequently because he never goes hunting but even if he did, I think it unlikely that he would be successful. His size and tail deficiency has tended to make him a somewhat clumsy cat in comparison with those smaller and daintier and with a full complement of tail. Any mouse worth its salt would be clear away when he heard Bumble crashing through the undergrowth.

He is, however, frequently in contact with the many sick and injured birds

which people bring to us and never has
he attacked them. He will often curl up
by the cage of a sick bird which has been
placed under a heater and indeed I have
known young birds to settle close to the
warmth of his ample back when missing
the warmth and comfort of the nest.

I am not for one moment suggesting
that Bumble has the welfare of the birds
at heart - he is simply taking advantage
of their heater but I do think that he
accepts that they are my birds and for
that reason they are not to be harmed.

I shall always remember one particular
occasion when I had reared a little
nestling swift. It so happened that it was
necessary for me to be away all day and
I was a little worried that the day would
be too long for the tiny creature and
when I returned late that evening, it did
indeed look somewhat droopy.

I wrapped it lightly in a chiffon scarf
and held it in my hand as I sat before
the fire thinking to warm it properly
before I went to bed. Bumble sat on
the arm of my chair watching as usual.

Because I was so tired I dropped off to
sleep and waking, about an hour later, I
found Bumble settled in my lap with his
beautiful, great head across my arm and
the hand which held the little swift.

I thought what an odd trio we made -
three separate species with no words to
communicate and yet in that moment
completely united in the absence of
intent to harm - which was a kind of
love I suppose.

This is the dove
of love and peace, not heartless love
the lancer.

        Edwin Muir - *Song*

This is the story then, of my dear Bumble. I know that I have not done justice to him but the communication between us has always been unspoken and is therefore almost impossible to put into words that others may understand.

Of all the cats which, during the course of my work I have come to know either briefly or intimately, Bumble stands alone - unique and irreplaceable.

Sometimes, in the evenings when I am relaxing in an armchair deciding what the rest of the evenings should hold or perhaps just listening to the silence, Bumble will jump up and putting his paws round my neck and his head under my chin, he will sigh once or twice and in no time at all be fast asleep. Such moments are a treasured delight to me - the knowledge of the complete affection and confidence of this dear old cat. I cannot claim to understand the processes of thought and reasoning within, what we choose to think of as the limitations of the mind of an animal, but my heart tells me that at such times Bumble's world is complete.

It has always seemed a wonder to me that we specks of humanity on a whirling world in an endless universe, by apparent chance, meet and for our short span know the comfort of complete union with another human being. That same chance, through all the time of eternity brought Bumble and I together.

When we both go our separate ways is it too fanciful to hope that our meeting will not have been to no purpose?

Is there perhaps, somewhere beyond our imagination, a harvest home of love which continues to refuel the core of caring and understanding which, against almost insurmountable odds, continues to exist in our world?